To

_____

(feel free to insert *me*)

on the occasion of your having a really Duh! day.

from

_____

on

_____

The Book of Duh

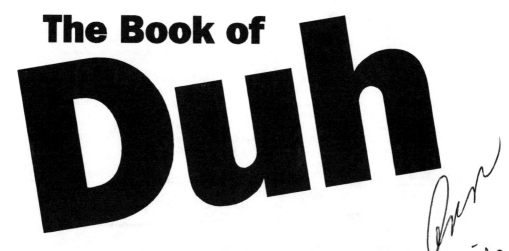

by Charlene Ann Baumbich

Harold Shaw Publishers
Wheaton, Illinois

Charlene Ann Baumbich

Portions of this book have been adapted and used by permission from:

Mama Said There'd Be Days Like This, © 1995 by Charlene Ann Baumbich. Published by Servant Publications, Box 8617, Ann Arbor, Michigan, 48107. Used with permission.

Don't Miss Your Kids! by Charlene Ann Baumbich. © 1991 by Charlene Ann Baumbich. Used by permission of InterVarsity Press, P.O. Box 1400, Downers Grove, IL 60515.

All Scripture quotations, unless otherwise indicated, are taken from the HOLY BIBLE, NEW INTERNATIONAL VERSION®. NIV® Copyright © 1973, 1978, 1984 International Bible Society. Used by permission of Zondervan Publishing House. All rights reserved.

ISBN 0-87788-060-3

Cover design by David LaPlaca

Library of Congress Cataloging-in-Publication Data

Baumbich, Charlene Ann, 1945-
    The book of duh : celebrating those less than magic moments / Charlene Baumbich.
        p.   cm.
    ISBN 0-87788-060-3
    1. Stupidity—Anecdotes.   2. Insight—Anecdotes.   3. Stupidity—Humor.   4. Insight—Humor.   I Title.
BF431.B3538 1997
155.2'32—dc21   97-20096
                                                                                             CIP

03   02   01   00   99   98   97
10   9   8   7   6   5   4   3   2   1

This book is dedicated to Victor Wilson Brown,
who taught me how to laugh at myself.
Thanks, Dad, for that magnificent blessing.
I love you.

Your favorite daughter.

Acknowledgments

Thanks to my family and friends who trust me enough to send me their stories or let me tell their stories, and who love me—even after I tell mine.

Especially thanks for laughing with me and not at me. (That is what you're doing, isn't it?)

Duh! Welcome

Perhaps you've just experienced your own Duh! moment. Or maybe you would like to give this book as a consolation to someone else recovering from a Duh! Either way, the fact that you're reading this leads me to believe we can already relate.

It's somewhat intimidating writing the "official" *Book of Duh!* even though in many ways I believe I was *born* to write this book. But if this is *the* book of Duh! what makes me think I'm qualified?

Honest answer? I followed me around for a day—I'm the queen of Duh! moments. And a brief survey of my friends reinforced my self-proclaimed queenship. Why, a while back, my good friend Carolyn Noorbakhsh even gave me a T-shirt for my birthday that said, "A legend in her own mind." Alas, I guess you could say that in this book I'm giving out the secret building blocks I've used to obtain that funny (you did mean it that way, didn't you, Carolyn?) gift.

A Helpful Hint

The term *Duh!* will be interchanged liberally with *Doink!*, *Whack up the side of the head!*, *Hel-LO!*, and other versions of Duh! to keep us all from going crazy. Often the Duh! will simply be implied within the story lest this book have its own moment of, "Duh! Do you think we've used too many *Duhs?*"

Duh! Mission Statement

I hope this small book will help you learn to celebrate those Duh! moments and realize that you're not alone.

Explanation of the Duh! Mission Statement

Just imagine if we never had Duh! moments. We would be Duh!-less. We would *never* get the point. We would, in fact, go through life clueless when the clues are so obvious we are tripping all over them.

And so it is that we should relish, welcome, and celebrate those whack-up-the-side-of-the-head encounters when understanding finally dawns, when we realize something we should have known but didn't. Or perhaps something we simply forgot for a spell.

All Duh! moments should be followed by a big ol' grin and a "Thanks be to God!" for our enlightenment. Otherwise, all we are left with is embarrassment.

Duh! "Official" Definition

(from Her Reigning Highness)

DUH! An awakening to:

1) your momentary lapse of memory
2) an observer's recognition of your momentary lapse of memory which he or she cannot help pointing out to you by exclaiming Duh!
3) a new thought that should have been an old thought
4) a guttural sound that bursts from your mouth when you recognize your own temporary stupidity
5) an instant, powerful awakening in your soul to a truth that you know must be accepted.

1
Let Duh Stories Begin!

George and I were traveling Illinois toll roads; he was driving. The change for tolls was in a compartment on my side of the car, so each time George held his hand out for forty cents, I handed him a quarter, a dime, and a nickel. A quarter, a dime, and a nickel. A quarter, a dime, and a nickel. After several tolls, I suddenly discovered I was running low on change.

As we were nearing the gate, almost too late to change lanes, I barked, "You'll have to go through the manual line. I'm out of exact change!"

"You don't have forty cents left?"

"No. I've only got four dimes."

"But four dimes *is* forty cents!"

The blessing here is that if George hadn't awakened my idling brain, we might be deaf today, after being honked into oblivion by truck drivers as we tried to snake our way across four lanes of traffic—exactly forty cents in hand.

For creatures of habit, it is at times nearly impossible to envision any other way of doing things. Sometimes it takes publicly embarrassing moments to make us see alternate possibilities. Such was the case for a friend of mine during one of the years when fashion changed back (yet again) from bell bottoms to near peg-leg pants.

My friend Marlene Minor puzzled aloud to her coworkers about how we would be able to negotiate pulling our socks on under the slacks when there was barely breathing space for our ankles. Bear in mind that Marlene headed a two-million dollar budget and managed thirty-five employees.

"Marlene," her coworker said. "You put your socks on *first.*"

Something to Celebrate:

Without the Duh!, Marlene might still be rolling around on the floor today, socks in hand, trying to accomplish the impossible.

My friend Ann Spangler is a topnotch writer and editor. She is a respected businesswoman with a great sense of humor and a new baby daughter. She is a woman I trust to have good judgment, thereby proving that any of us can be fooled. (Just kidding, Ann.)

During a recent drive she was surprised to find herself suddenly bothered by allergy symptoms. The desert is not known to cause such symptoms, and since her move to a hot, dry climate a couple of years ago, Ann had been relatively allergy free. But sure enough, here she was suffering those pesky symptoms she recognized from all her years in the Midwest. It felt like her sinuses were being squeezed, and her eyes and head got that familiar achy feeling.

Then, much to her chagrin, she noticed something about the new headband she was wearing—it was too tight. The minute Ann removed it, her "allergies" miraculously cleared up.

I pulled up to the speaker at a drive-through window outside a fast-food restaurant. "I'd like four hamburgers with everything, two large fries, and two medium diet colas. That's to go, please."

Doink!

I was in a fancy restaurant trying to eat like a lady when I noticed that a major dollop of lumpy blue cheese sauce had escaped from my hot wing and landed on my chest. Rather than draw attention to myself by daintily wiping the area with a napkin—which always leaves a smear—I decided I'd just flick the sauce away.

Of course I didn't catch it just right; rather than being whisked away, the morsel plopped into my lap after leaving a gooey inch-wide ribbon on my chest. I sighed and discreetly attempted to flick it off my lap, which now had its own blue cheese streak. Instead of disappearing, the sauce rolled down my pant leg, leaving a snowball's white trail. I kicked my leg, and the blob rolled into the top of my shoe where it parked, after having oozed across the top of my dark sock.

My desire to avoid a smear and not to draw attention to myself led to a royal failure. Now I didn't need a napkin; I needed a hose and a shower.

A General Thought:

We will all have embarrassing, dreadful moments. Hel-LO! This is a Bible promise, folks: "In this world you will have trouble" (John 16:33).

But the rest of that passage is what we often forget, and it strikes like a lightning bolt of Duh! when we remember. This promise can change the course of our response to all situations: "But take heart! I have overcome the world."

Electronics. Love 'em. Hate 'em. We purchased a new dryer several months ago. I thought I'd been a responsible shopper, not only shopping for price, but also asking all the important questions. I thought I'd made the perfect choice.

The dryer is in our basement. For me to be doing laundry and working in my office at the same time, I have to come up from the basement into the garage, then up from the garage into the kitchen (we have a bi-level), then from the kitchen up to my office. Soon after the new dryer arrived, I discovered that I cannot hear the buzzer on it the way I could hear the old one, and that it only buzzes a few times before it turns off, rather than tumbling for a very long time as my old dryer used to do. Alas, my permanent press clothes started getting permanently wrinkled because I wasn't getting them out at the sound of the buzz. What to do? What to do? Certainly not use the iron! I ended up putting the clothes back in the dryer again with a damp cloth. Not exactly environmental economics, huh?

One day it struck me that I could get an intercom! So I went shopping, comparing prices, and asking all the right questions. I ended up buying a baby room monitor. Brilliant! I put the baby end on top of my dryer and the listening end in my office.

Not long after this, George was out of town for the weekend, and I was working in my office while doing laundry. Suddenly I heard a man's voice over the intercom. Yikes! My heart began to race. He was speaking in a quiet, droning voice. I crept down the stairs to the kitchen to lock the door to the garage and then flee the house, phone the police, and have the intruder arrested.

Suddenly it hit me: The guy was still droning on, and he was talking about sales figures. My baby monitor had picked up someone's cordless phone!

Even though I'd heard about things like this on the news, it was the first time I had seen and heard such irrefutable evidence that we never know who's listening. So watch out, it might even be ME!

Our babies are grown and gone, but George and I still carve pumpkins every Halloween. After years of scooping the pulp out the top and wrangling around trying to either set lit candles inside or submerge a lit match into the cavern, one day I was watching a television program that revolutionized our task.

Some genius discovered that you can also carve from the bottom of the pumpkin! Hel-LO! All you have to do to light up for the evening is set the pumpkin top aside, place the candle on the ground, light the candle, and set the pumpkin over the top! Remember folks, you learned it here, in *The Book of Duh!*

My trucker friend Tom Stewart e-mailed me this true story. Tom was driving a big rig at the time.

A couple of years ago I was making a delivery in Maine, and I asked the dockhand (picture a weathered fisherman-type, complexion like old leather) how best to get to my next stop. He looked at my rig and thought about it for a while. Maine is, of course, not built for a large truck, and most of the roads are very narrow and meet themselves coming back.

Finally, the dockhand looked up and said in his long New England drawl, "Weeealll, you caint get theah . . . from heeah!"

George Burns was a great storyteller with an impeccable gift of comedic timing. I hesitate to try and retell one of his little ditties, but I believe the thought definitely belongs in this book. This is the gist of what I remember.

George Burns developed a terrible cough. He went from one doctor to another, paying high bills and trying different medications, but nothing worked.

Then one day someone recommended this funny little neighborhood physician who charged very cheap fees. Mr. Burns wondered how good he could possibly be but thought visiting him might be worth a shot since nothing else seemed to work.

After Mr. Burns unfolded the entire history of his cough, the doctor looked at him and said, "Stop coughing."

George Burns said, "So I did."

2

Duhsn't It Make You Crazy When . . .

. . . your electricity is off due to a power outage and you keep walking over to the light switch and flipping it anyway?

. . . your water is turned off and you still keep turning on the faucet or flushing the toilet?

. . . you run to your basement to get . . . ?

. . . you run to your bedroom to get . . . ?

. . . you run to the bathroom to . . . (never mind).

. . . you pick up your hot curling iron by the wrong end?

. . . you phone someone and can't remember who, so you just begin rapid-fire chatting, hoping to recognize the voice?

. . . you get to work and discover you're wearing two unmatched socks or shoes?

. . . you're out with your spouse and another couple and you give your honey that gentle kick under the table that says, "Don't GO there," only to have him or her say, in a very loud voice, "Why are you kicking me?"

. . . you can't remember if you took your pills or not?

. . . you get a cast off your leg but you keep limping anyway?

. . . you get cable television but keep watching mindless network programs out of habit?

. . . you search everywhere for your glasses, then find them on top of your head?

. . . you rent a movie and realize ten seconds into it that you've rented it before?

... someone keeps reminding you that you do these things time and time again?

... you swat a mosquito that has landed on your nose and give yourself a nose bleed?

... you think your remote control is broken, then realize you're trying to change channels with the cordless phone?

... you realize you're using the wrong toothbrush?

... you pick up your glass, go to slip your lip over the edge for a big gulp, then have a straw poke you in the eye?

... you pick up your glass, your mouth gropes for the straw and there isn't one?

... you wipe your mouth with your napkin, then realize it's the tail of your blouse?

... you continue to do all three of the above in restaurants during business meetings?

There was an old retired couple, seasoned citizens. The man was going out and asked his wife if she wanted him to bring anything back.

She said that they needed bread and milk for breakfast and that she would write it down for him.

He protested that there were only two items, bread and milk, and that he could remember them. Irritated that she would doubt his memory, he left muttering to himself, bread and milk, bread and milk. . . .

Upon his return he presented her with a sack containing bacon and eggs.

She looked inside and said, "I knew I should have written a list. You forgot the butter!"

Or how about the three ladies talking about their memories: One complained that she was forgetting things. She said that sometimes in normal conversation she would completely forget what she was talking about.

The second lady complained of a similar problem. She would be driving to town for something and forget what she was going after or where she was going, and she would have to turn around and go home.

The third lady said that she never had any problems like that and rapped the table, muttering "knock on wood." Immediately she added, "Would you excuse me? I have to answer the door."

(The above two jokes were e-mailed to me by my friend Tom Stewart. They just seemed to fit.)

A couple of months ago I was going through a particularly stressful time. I had a luncheon engagement in downtown Chicago, and I took the commuter train, as I usually do when I visit the city. It offers a great opportunity to simply sit a spell and catch my breath; time to change gears before my arrival at a destination.

My friend Rhonda Reese had recently given me one of the swell, small Bibles, and I'd put it in my purse to use at such free moments. Good time to inhale, exhale, get some quiet time. When the train reached the downtown station, I was completely calm.

But then I arrived at the luncheon, and someone immediately made the mistake of asking me how I was. (What *were* they thinking?) As I recited in detail all the reasons for my stress, I finally revved myself back into a tizzy—a state which I surely must enjoy since I was so anxious to recapture it.

That mini saga has a couple of powerful Duh! points. I became calm when I read my Bible. (Hel-LO! I know this. Why do I not go there

first?) I lathered myself—I lathered *myself*—back into an anxious state when I dwelt on my stress.

I only hope I remember that in the future; I'm afraid I've even said *that* way too many times in the past.

Duh! moments often happen because we activate our actions before activating our brains. My friend Rhonda Reese told me about the day she decided to clean. Really clean.

"I stood up on a table to dust the ceiling fan—which happened to be turned on—and it whacked the top of my head and knocked me flat as a flitter. Right off the table, rump first, onto the floor. Confirmed my belief: Housework is dangerous."

This is profound. I agree with her. No more cleaning. I believe that fan knocked some sense into her.

I am not repeating this information to my husband; I'll just wait to see if he notices my new brilliant non-plan. Of course I doubt he'd be too shocked since I'm the one who suggested sprinkling glitter on the cobwebs. Wouldn't that be beautiful?

39

How often do we hear people (including ourselves) say something like this: "My friend in California called me on the phone the other day."

Think about it. How *else* would she call you? With a primal scream heard 'round the world?

?!

My friend Paul Halvey says one of his personal favorite Duh!s is the little box printed on envelopes showing us where we should put the stamp. "As if that weren't bad enough," he said, "some companies feel compelled to include a message in the box, such as 'The Post Office will not deliver mail without a stamp.'"

I heard a story about a woman who suffered a flat tire while driving her van; alas, try as she might, she could find no spare tire to use. She called a roadway service, told them her problem, and waited for them to come tow her to a service station.

Upon arrival, the service station worker told her the tire was beyond repair, which she already suspected, and sold her a replacement tire.

When her husband arrived home that evening, she told him the tale of her terrible day. That's when he walked her outside and pointed to the back of the van door—right where the spare tire was encased in that big round tire-shaped place.

My deep-thinking friend, Paul Halvey, sent me the following e-mail one day.

Have you ever looked at those fancy, high-tech plumbing fixtures in public rest rooms? The ones that turn the water off or flush the commode when you step away? I'll bet you thought, "There's a high-tech plumber somewhere who wanted to improve the equipment with the latest technology."

Wrong. This invention isn't an effort to raise the standard, but to make bathrooms idiot-resistant for those folk who haven't figured out that you still ought to turn off fixtures, even if they aren't yours."

To this I would say, good point, Paul, but that wasn't my first thought. My first thought was, where is that electronic eye aimed so that it triggers the flush when I'm rising up off the toilet? I even heard

42

of a family whose child almost abandoned toilet training after going on a trip where every rest stop was equipped with these devices. Their wiggly child triggered the flush as soon as she sat down and repositioned herself on the too-big seat; then she would bound up, scared by the flush, so the thing would flush again. Then she sat down again . . . you can figure out the rest.

My second thought was, if these sinks are supposed to automatically turn off to save water, why do they waste water turning on and off while I'm just standing there trying to comb my hair?

Several of my friends subscribe to a voice-mail service provided by one of the telephone companies. Many came to this after battling the limitations of answering machines—as in the machine's inability to answer when you're on the phone, tapes going bad, power outages, stuff like that.

Nothing is without flaws, however. Two different friends reported the following situation with voice mail: People began asking them why they hadn't returned their calls. It seems my friends didn't even know these people had left messages. So they each phoned the voice mail service to complain that they weren't getting all their messages.

Guess what question the phone company wanted answered so they could investigate? "What day and what time did your friends leave their messages?"!

I was out of town on a two-night speaking engagement. By the end of the second night I was really tuckered out. I was quite happy to fall into bed early in my hotel room, looking forward to a nice leisurely morning shower and a peaceful breakfast before I packed up for the drive home.

I slept well, waking up refreshed. After my shower, I headed downstairs to the complimentary breakfast buffet. As it happened, I was the only one in the room, and I was blissfully enjoying the silence, the orange juice, the scrambled eggs, the fried potatoes, the grits, the bacon, the . . . .

A gentleman who worked at the place walked into the room and headed straight for the television. He switched it on and said, "This will give you something to do while you eat." Before I could swallow and open my mouth to object, he was gone.

Bad news. Violence. Storms. Trials. Suspects. War zones.

Hel-LO! I had something to do before he entered and opened the gates to the evils of the world: Enjoy the blessed silence.

3

Meet Duh Family

Parents, especially mothers, seem to be born with a stock pile of big Hel-LOs! in their genes. How else can we explain the fact that we stick our fingers in diapers to check for messes?

Say what? Your husband forgets birthdays? Leaves dirty underwear on the bathroom floor where he stepped out of them? Has this annoying habit of rattling his change in his pocket? Falls asleep in his lounge chair while you're talking to him? Duh! What did you think the "for worse" part of your wedding vows really meant?

The Blessing:
If that's as "for worse" as it ever gets, that's pretty darn good.

?!

Rebuttal.
Say what? Your wife uses your razor to shave her legs? Leaves fast-food wrappers on the floor of the family car after driving the kids around all day? Doesn't know a lug nut from a luggage rack? Talks

to you nonstop when there's ten seconds left to the game and it's fourth down with one yard to go?

(See the previous Blessing.)

When our two boys were young, we occasionally ate dinner in a restaurant. You know, Family Night Out. (This happened as often as I could humanly convince my husband.) It was usually fast food or very casual dining.

One evening when Brian was about seven years old, we were gathered around a restaurant table that had actual cloth napkins. Suddenly Brian held up his fork and said, in a very loud voice, "Who's missing a fork? I've got two of them."

Ms. Manners would have fainted dead away.

Aunt Sally was my grandma Lander's older sister. I remember these things about her: She wore a handmade night cap on her head when retiring for the evening. It covered her long, wound-around hair. She was a quiet, beautiful, hard-working, praying, and gentle soul I loved being around. She was not funny. Except for one time.

I was about fourteen years old and Aunt Sally had come all the way from Texas to visit Grandma and Grandpa in Illinois. Looking back on it, I realize she had probably come to help and support my grandmother—my grandfather was failing fast from cancer of the esophagus. The mood around the house was anything but silly.

Aunt Sally was vacuuming with Grandma's canister-type sweeper. Boy was she vacuuming. Here and there. Under and around. In between and on top. I was watching television and occasionally glancing at Aunt Sally out of the corner of my eye. After a while I noticed her giving a few swipes in one particular spot, then swiping again. Then again, covering exactly the same place but very slowly this time. Then

she just stood motionless while the sweeper lapped at the same spot for an extended time. By now she had my full attention—and I began to laugh.

Aunt Sally didn't hear me because the sweeper was running, and besides her full attention was on her job. Pulling back from her mission, she squatted down to inspect the floor, nearly planting her nose into the carpet nap. I saw her mouth move and then she tilted the hose back and put her hand across the bottom of the suctioning area. Meanwhile, I was soundlessly busting a gut!

Finally she turned around to switch off the sweeper, and what to her wondering eyes should appear but—NOTHING! She'd "vacuumed" practically the entire living room while the canister sat back in the dining room unattached to her hose. There Aunt Sally stood, Hose to Nowhere in her hands.

The blessing in this moment, even for Aunt Sally, was that soon Grandma, via our retelling of the incident and my unleashed, hysterical

53

guffawing, was enveloped in much-needed, refreshing, bountiful glee. It was one of those priceless Duh! moments we all need sometimes, when we are able to put aside our pride, gain some perspective, and simply wallow in the laughter.

George and I were on vacation, and we spent the night in a motel. In the morning I crawled out of bed and announced to George, "I hardly slept at all. You were snoring all night!"

"I didn't sleep either," he replied.

What's wrong with this picture?

George and I were engaged in the lively art of conversation when he stopped talking for a moment and retrieved his white, no-frills cloth hanky out of his back pocket. He unfolded it and vigorously blew his nose. I mean honking blew his nose. George is a serious nose blower. I continued to talk without skipping a beat.

After several good snorts, George folded the hanky right on the creases until it was returned to its most perfect original square. Then, holding it in his left hand, he slid the hanky down into his back pocket.

When he looked up at me, I had suddenly become mute—a most unnatural state for me. My mouth was agape. I couldn't believe what I was seeing, and it showed on my face.

"Is something wrong?" George asked.

"Do you always fold your hanky like that after you blow your nose?"

"Yes. Is that a problem?"

"Maybe."

"Now what?"

56

"I hate to tell you this, George, but after twenty-five years of married life, I had no idea you folded your hanky back up like that after blowing your nose."

"So . . . ?"

"So, I'm sorry to tell you that when I'm doing laundry and I find the hanky so neatly folded in your back pocket, I assume it hasn't been used, and I simply put it back in your drawer without washing it."

It was George's turn to stand with his mouth agape. After a couple of beats passed, he responded, "No wonder I always have so much trouble getting my glasses clean."

The Blessing:

If we are still making discoveries like this after twenty-five years of marriage, who knows what surprises are in store for the next twenty-five years?

see, it runs in the family. . . .

My dad told me about the day he picked up new glasses. He took them off when he left the doctor's office and slid them into his shirt pocket.

Then he noticed his shoe was untied so he bent over to secure it. Of course, his glasses fell out, lenses to the sidewalk. When Dad moved forward and bent over to pick them up, he accidentally kicked them and they skittered and scratched their way farther down the sidewalk. He caught up with them, moved forward, bent over to pick them up, and accidentally kicked them again! They were ruined before he got into his car.

And then . . .

George and I were going to watch a slide show and video presentation of our nephew's several-month working stay in Alaska. I looked all over for my glasses and finally found them in a dumb spot in the bathroom. Off we went.

Upon arrival, I realized I'd left the glasses at home! They weren't in my purse, and they weren't on top of my head (a place I often find them when I'm looking for them); they weren't anywhere. George responded in a very kind fashion to the latest of my seemingly unending fiascos with glasses. I checked his shirt to see if there was blood running down the front of it from his biting his tongue so hard. Then I sat and watched the entire evening's presentation through the haze of my midlife eyes.

When we were getting in the car to leave, I stuck my hand in my coat pocket. Guess what I found?

And I remember when . . .

Our older son, Bret, needed glasses in grammar school. He lost his first pair within a few days in a giant mud hole near a construction zone. No amount of mud wrestling produced them. We had to get replacements.

When he got contact lenses, they told us to come back in two weeks to see how he was handling them. In three days he'd lost them—out of his eyes! He was walking along a busy street near our home, and a semi-truck whipped by, kicking up dust and a whirlwind. Bret rubbed his eyes, and the contacts both flew out into the weeds, never to be seen again.

And finally . . .

Our younger son broke three pairs of expensive aviator sunglasses he needed to wear for flying lessons.

It seems the Queen of Duh! has inherited her glasses-related genes and passed them on. Does this make us Duh Royal Family?

4

On the Topic of Duh!

My husband left me the following note. "Your editor called about the book of Dah!"

I received a letter from a friend telling me she'd forgotten to have me do something the last time I was in her area. She ended this thought with, "Dah! Or is it Da?"

I received this e-mail from John Sadler after asking my friends if they had any Duh! moments they'd like to share. Keep in mind that John is an agronomist; he's highly intelligent, has a great sense of humor; he's a good writer, husband, father, and lots of other cool stuff. John also has a very large vocabulary and knows how to wield it.

Charstar,

I'm afraid our instincts toward self-preservation cause us to try to forget the Duh! moments as soon as humanly possible. However, now we are on notice that there is a use for them after the shock wears off.

Previously, the only known value of a Duh! moment to those of us mortals not creative enough to compile a compendium was the purported therapeutic value to the exasperated retelling of such Duh! moments, usually followed by our comments on the dunce that initiated the event.

Michelle Elliott has a kind and respectful way of saying Duh! to her mother, Kay. Rather than embarrassing her mom during one of Kay's mental hiccups by hollering Duh! she politely says, "Thanks for playing, Mom." I *like* this. (Hear that, family?)

5

Duh! upon Duh!

Occasionally I deliver Meals on Wheels as part of an ongoing service project of my Kiwanis group. Upon my arrival to pick up meals one day, Carol, the woman in charge of this much-needed senior assistance program, helped me carry the many insulated bags and boxes to my car. While we loaded, Carol grumbled that someone had carelessly erred and caused her a lot of trouble that morning. In fact, she was still running behind and feeling frustrated by it.

Suddenly, before I could open my mouth to say "Don't close the trunk!" Carol closed the trunk.

"Carol! My keys were in there!"

"I didn't think anyone set their keys in the trunk!"

Well, guess again. Now it was my turn to grumble—to myself, of course. *Didn't people ask if it is okay to close the trunk? Isn't that just common sense?*

"I always put my keys in the trunk when I'm loading it so I know where they are." Now we were both in a hurry, due to errors of other people! Haughtily I said to myself, *Guess we're all human, right Carol?*

Since the food was hot and cold and was supposed to stay that way until it was delivered, we needed to get active. We concluded that Carol would drive me home to get the extra set of car keys George and I have the good sense to keep handy just in case.

I made a deliberate point of locking my car doors with the auto-door lock button before we left it abandoned in the parking lot. I hopped in Carol's car, and off we went toward my house. My house that was locked. My house that required either an electronic garage door opener or a set of keys to open. And you know where those items were. This didn't occur to *me,* however, until we'd entered my driveway.

"Oh no, Carol. I locked my car and the opener was in there! I'll have to call a locksmith!"

Now, it was Carol's turn to grumble, silently of course. *Guess we're all human, right Charlene?*

Back to the food center we went. Just as we were about to enter the building to make the phone call, a local police officer marking tires for possible parking violations came by.

"Could you help me?" I asked. "I locked my keys in the trunk." In short order she had me inside the car. I grabbed the garage door opener and again Carol drove me to my house to get the extra set of keys for the trunk. I could picture the faces of all those hungry people trying to pry open their doors in their weakened, food-deprived state as I delivered them melted and lukewarm delicacies.

Finally, off I went on my route. People were not angry; they expressed concern for me and thankfulness for the meal, and I was blessed by their words of encouragement.

Later that day I was telling a friend about the comedy of errors. Her reply delivered another smashing blow to my ego and one of the day's biggest Duh!s. "Don't you have a button inside your car that unlocks the trunk?"

"Yes, but I'd locked my car, remember?"

"But not until you decided to depart for your house to get the extra keys, right?"

Right!

There was a writing project I wanted to submit to a couple of major magazines for publication, but I just couldn't seem to trip the trigger. It was seasonal material, so the clock was ticking. Every day I'd say, "I'm *sending* that story today," but odds and ends seemed to eat away all my time, and it wouldn't get sent. To make it worse, I cared particularly about this piece and really wanted it to find an audience. I hate when I get in this cycle of not getting done what I want to—especially when there's no one else to blame.

Finally, I called my friend Larry Turner who was familiar with the piece and had encouraged me to submit it. I wanted to talk over this temporary behavioral dysfunction I was suffering. (Notice I was now making phone calls rather than sending the piece.) I needed an opinion as to whether or not I had some kind of deep psychological block.

I unfolded the saga to Larry, then finally wound myself down.

"Just do it," he suggested.

71

"You're right!" I yelped. I have brilliant friends, don't I? The thought that I could *just do it* whacked me up the side of the head as though I'd never heard such an idea before.

While I was busy thanking Larry for his counsel, I surveyed my desk, looking for the paperwork. I also noticed that my glass of water was completely empty. "See, Larry?" I cried. "I'm already dreaming up other things I have to do first. I have to go fill my water glass, then I'll begin. What's wrong with me?"

"Why don't you see how much you can get done without water?" he replied.

Wow! Another Doink! It just never occurs to me to do without. At this point I began laughing because I knew I was activated. I thanked him yet again, hung up the phone, wrote my cover letters, and even mailed them. I've yet to hear from the magazines as of this writing, but I continue to live in wonder at how often the obvious just needs to be stated.

On the topic of e-mail, I recently had to make an emergency trip out of town to assist with a family crisis. Being one who finds writing cathartic and who enjoys ongoing correspondences with several on-line buddies and buddettes, I took my computer so I could stay connected with the healthy side of my psyche (assuming that I have one), my family, and my friends.

While I was gone I began to encounter an increase in my blood pressure, which previous to this trip had already been making itself known. What I didn't need was to worry about my own health since the crisis itself took all my energies. So, along with updating my friends as to how things were going, I sent out on-line prayer requests to friends I know are faithful prayer warriors.

(Something you must know here is that I have the ability to try and take charge of all details. Sometimes this is good; sometimes this is bad. It is very bad when I try to manage details that are beyond my control and/or that are not mine to be managing. Duh! Fretting and hand-wringing are in my vocabulary and my behavior when I don't check them. I was falling into this during my emergency trip, and it was not helping my blood pressure!)

Suddenly three of the people I asked to pray for me all began giving me the same advice—advice that ran against my natural, knee-jerk instincts. I snorted about it the first time I read it. Grumbled out loud the second time I read it, and nearly flew into a hissy the third time.

Then, in a head-banging, God-filled Duh! of a moment, it struck me like lightning that if I had asked all these people to pray and they each were praying for me to get the same message (which wasn't what I'd asked for), I'd be a fool not to listen. My prayer was obviously already being answered in chorus! So I began to pray to *accept* the answer, which included letting go and letting God handle the details.

How many times? How many times will it take before the obvious and the answer register on the first go-around?

was baking a cake the other day while trying to do several other tasks. One of the tasks was making a phone call to an editor. While we were on the phone, I realized my oven timer was dinging.

"Can you hold on a moment, please? My cake timer is dinging." (This is an editor with whom I have a friendly relationship. Since she is also a she, I thought she'd understand.)

I ran downstairs and picked up my other phone to continue the conversation, turned off the dinger, rustled through a drawer for my hot mitts, looked at the cake, and decided it needed another minute.

We continued our chat for a moment, and then I realized I needed to run upstairs to look at my notes. Before I reached the second step, I remembered I'd put the cake back in the oven, so I picked up the downstairs phone again and said, "I didn't reset this timer, so I better stay right here or I'll forget I've got this cake in the oven. I know me."

When I glanced through the glass door to spy on the cake, though, I realized I hadn't turned off the dinger, I'd turned off the oven! I turned it back on, noticing at the same time that I'd wound myself up in the phone cord. When I had succeeded in unwinding myself, I decided to take the cake out—done or not—but I couldn't find where I'd put the hot pads.

Finally I got the cake pans out of the oven, and, really needing to find my notes so I could complete the phone conversation, I simply set the pans down on the burners on top of the stove and ran upstairs. That's when I remembered I hadn't turned the oven off and the burners were going to be hot. Then . . . you get the picture.

I'd like to take this moment to thank Joan Guest, the editor, for hanging in there with me. Fortunately, she's the editor of *this* book and understands that authors are always encouraged to write what they know.

Her kind words to me at the end of this cycle were, "You're right. You *are* the Queen of Duh!"

6

Double Duh!

George and I were vacationing in Oregon and found ourselves at Cannon Beach along the Pacific coast. When nature called me (I mean with one of those serious, right-now! calls), I queried George as to whether he might have noticed any restroom signs.

"There's a sign right there," he said, pointing up at a signpost. The sign read *Restrooms East,* but there was no arrow.

"Which way is east?" I asked.

"I don't know," he replied, at which point we both began reciting, "The sun rises in the east and sets in the west" while looking up at the sky. But it was overcast—no sun; no help. My "call" began to reach a critical point, so we had to activate another approach.

George (thank goodness it wasn't me) asked a passerby if he could point us to the east, a.k.a. the restrooms.

"Well," the man replied with a grin, then a slight pause, "The ocean is there, so . . ."

Double Duh!

There are several reasons I was happy for this moment. The first is obvious; my situation was critical. The second reason is more ambiguous, but consider this: What if we determined east was *in* the ocean? (Remember those childhood swimming days?) Finally, once again we were given an opportunity to realize how much useful information we already have in our own brains—all we have to do is find it there.

Mickey Jackson and I were on a much-needed retreat her church was sponsoring. The topic was prayer. We were roommates—two responsible working women who had escaped our usual duties for the weekend. Seems we also parked our brains; you be the judge.

The first night our room was warm. The heating system, over which we had no control, was set on melt. So we cracked the window and slept well, enjoying the fresh air. The second night, however, the temperature dropped, and the heat to the room seemed missing. Still, having enjoyed the nice cool air the night before, we cranked open our window. (Feel it coming?) Of course we spent the night freezing in our twin beds, clutching the sheets and thin bedspreads around our chins. No blankets in sight.

Finally, Mickey got up and closed the window, but not until about three hours after we were frozen. Neither one of us slept very well the rest of the night, and we both grumbled about a lack of covers and the fact that the heating system was so erratic.

The next morning, our last morning on retreat, the announcement was made that we should strip our beds, leave the sheets in the hall, put the bedspreads back on the beds, and put the blankets back in the drawers.

Blankets? In the drawers?!

"Dear Lord," we said, having learned about prayer this weekend, "please help us be smarter."

Keepers of the Big Wheel Brigade" was the title justly earned by Mary Gingell and me one summer when her son Noah and my Brian were about three years old. It wasn't the only title we bore, nor was it the grandest I suppose, but we wore it proudly nevertheless.

I can picture us vividly. Mary's Dr. Scholl's sandals clip-clopping along the Gingells' blacktop driveway. Noah's pants that simply would not stay above the top of the crease in his slimmer-than-slim buttocks. Brian always, but always, wearing a baseball cap with his ears tucked inside. He also hiked his pants up a little too high and wore his belts a little too tight—a habit, thank goodness, which he outgrew before the word *geek* came along. And me. Well, I usually had a dish towel thrown over my shoulder, and Mary had to remind me about it.

That summer Mary and Hugh built a spacious, six-inch high deck right outside their front door and stained it red. Although that sounds a little peculiar—not the red but the six inches—it totally changed the

atmosphere: we now parked our lawn chairs on the deck instead of the blacktop driveway.

We spent a portion of almost every day on that deck watching the boys career their Big Wheels at very high speeds toward the street-end of the driveway, slam on the brakes, do a donut, and roar back toward us—those were memories number 5,003 through 6,003.

Day after day, time after time, Mary and I would take turns stopping our chatter mid-sentence to lunge after one of the boys who simply could not remember that we had told them, DON'T DRIVE TOO CLOSE TO THE STREET! This was weeks of launching ourselves. Actually months.

Although it probably wasn't bad for our cardiovascular systems, that electrifying zap that rushes through any mother when she fears her child will meet with peril before she can reach him surely felt stroke-inducing at times. But we endured and even managed to solve world problems, as well as catch a few rays, between launches.

Then one day, life as we knew it was altered in a divine flash of Duh! One of us, and I honestly can't remember who (but I hope it was me), was struck with a revelation: We would no longer need to live like astronauts if we just sat in our chairs at the *street* end of the driveway.

My friend Donna Chavez and I each acquired a new software program, first her, then me. As I progressed in my learning curve, I would occasionally solicit her sage advice.

One particular day I called to ask how in the world you could rename a folder. I'd tried everything. Now keep in mind that I've been working on a computer for about twelve years, so I'm familiar with at least the basics. I was perplexed that I couldn't figure this one out.

"Oh that's easy," she said. We each wore our headsets as we talked on the phone—aren't we high tech?—and she booted up to the same portion of the program I was looking at so we could do this together.

"You just . . . " she said.

"Doesn't work. Tried it."

"Sure it does."

She tried it. Didn't work.

"Okay," she continued, "you probably . . . "

"Doesn't work. Tried it."

Of course she tried each of the things I said didn't work, and they didn't work for her either. (I withhold a Duh! here.)

Donna went on to suggest a few things, and we tried them together. No go. Finally, we concluded that you simply could not change a folder name. Period.

Another friend of mine got the same software, and I sent her an e-mail congratulating her. I gave her a few hints about some of the cool little things this program could do, but I also filled her in on the programming flaw.

Not long afterward I saw this friend at a luncheon, and this is what she said to me, "Oh, you know how you said you couldn't rename the folder? Well, you just go to the File menu and select Rename Folder. I can't believe I'm telling YOU something about this program. I feel like such a genius!"

I sat contemplating how it could have been humanly possible for both Donna and me to miss something so obvious. This is how nearly

all the computer programs I know let you rename folders. Surely we hadn't missed this! I came right home and tried it. It worked.

I e-mailed Donna with this awakening of our stupidity. Her e-mail back was right on target: "Duh!"

I was in the middle of a very stressful chain of events, including several that had deadlines attached to them. You know, one of those spells we all have when we think that if just one more person asks something of us or one more thing goes wrong, our head will blow off.

And then one more person reminded me I had one more thing to do: it was my week of the month to wash sheets for the homeless shelter our church hosts. My first impulse, after listening to the phone message, was for my throat to tighten and my fists to clench.

Then a Duh! from heaven struck me like a lightning bolt. I am complaining about one more thing to do? Many of the things already on my plate have to do with steady work, friendship, good books, and a baptism. I have a job, a home to shelter me from the wind and world, words to edify my soul, people to pray for my stressful times, family to love, family to give me love, freedom to sit in my spacious yard any time I want, a car, arms to hold me when I weep, neighbors to count on and play with, telephones and televisions at nearly every elbow, a closet full of clothes, good music to soothe my psyche . . . health, hands, soap, a washer and dryer.

Dear Lord, I thought, *help me to be thankful for the bounty. Let me remember that I am in control of how much is crammed into my schedule. Let me yearn, with all that is in me, to honor your commands without grumbling. Allow me to remember that moments like these, which awaken me to the deepest, richest truths, are pure grace.*

The Mother of All Duh!s—and Duh! Conclusion

I am a lifelong Chicago Cub's fan.

Other books by Charlene Ann Baumbich:

Don't Miss Your Kids (they'll be gone before you know it)
How to Eat Humble Pie & Not Get Indigestion
Mama Said There'd Be Days Like This (but she never said just how many)
The 12 Dazes of Christmas (& One Holy Night)

How to contact The Queen of Duh:
Charlene Ann Baumbich
Phone: (630) 858-1091
Fax: (630) 858-1094
E-mail: Charstar1@Juno.com

She welcomes invitations to speak, compliments, and other people's Duh! moments. If you have a complaint, please share it with your pet. Do you think the Queen wants to listen to *those?* Duh!